S242 1921

W9-AUY-570

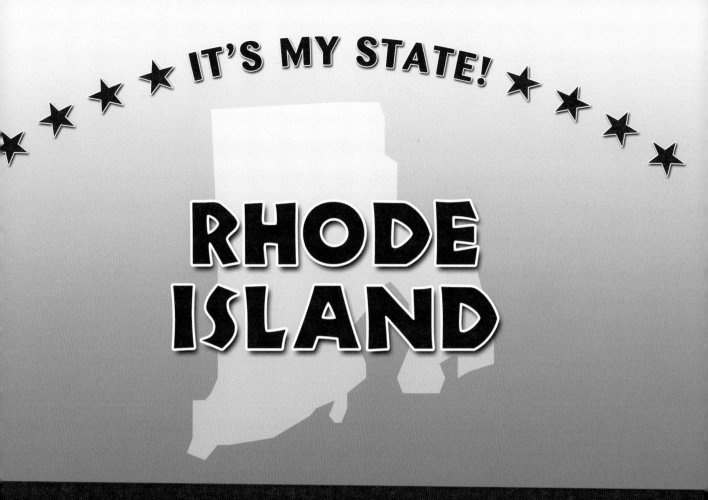

IT'S MY STATE!

RHODE ISLAND

Rick Petreycik

Lisa M. Herrington

Cavendish Square

New York

Published in 2014 by Cavendish Square Publishing, LLC
303 Park Avenue South, Suite 1247, New York, NY 10010

Library of Congress Cataloging-in-Publication Data
Petreycik, Rick.
          Rhode Island / Rick Petreycik, Lisa M. Herrington.
               p. cm. — (It's my state!)
          Summary: Surveys the history, geography, government, economy, and people of Rhode Island.
          Includes bibliographical references and index.
          ISBN 978-0-7614-8002-0 (hardcover) —ISBN 978-1-62712-103-3 (paperback)— ISBN 978-0-7614-8009-9 (ebook)
          1. Rhode Island—Juvenile literature. I. Herrington, Lisa M. II. Title. III. Series.
     F79.3.P48 2014
     974.5—dc23   2012024116

This edition developed for Cavendish Square Publishing by RJF Publishing LLC (www.RJFpublishing.com)
Series Designer, Second Edition: Tammy West/Westgraphix LLC

RHODE ISLAND

CONTENTS

THE OCEAN STATE

A Quick Look at
RHODE ISLAND

State Tree: Red Maple

The red maple, widespread in Rhode Island, was officially made the state tree in 1964. In the fall, its leaves turn brilliant colors of gold, purple, and red.

State Flower: Violet

Rhode Island was the last state to adopt an official state flower. Although schoolchildren chose the violet as the state flower in 1897, it did not officially become the state flower until 1968. Violets have striking deep purple or blue petals. They can be found in Rhode Islanders' gardens or growing wild in the state's fields and forests.

State Bird: Rhode Island Red

Rhode Island's state bird is actually a chicken. This special breed of chicken was introduced on a farm in the town of Little Compton in the 1850s. It was chosen as the state bird in 1954. The Rhode Island red is known for its tasty meat and eggs.

State Mineral: Bowenite

Bowenite is named after George Bowen, a Rhode Island geologist (a scientist who studies the layers of soil, rock, and minerals that make up Earth's crust). He discovered the mineral in the early 1800s. Similar to jade, bowenite is found mainly in northern sections of Rhode Island. This mineral typically ranges in color from green to yellow. Bowenite became the state mineral in 1966.

State Rock: Cumberlandite

Scientists estimate that cumberlandite rocks are a little more than one billion years old. The rocks are usually dark brown or black with white and gray markings. The state rock can be found around Narragansett Bay. Cumberlandite became the state's official rock in 1966. Cannonballs were made from this rock during the American Revolution (1775–1783).

State Shell: Quahog

The quahog is a thick-shelled, edible clam found along Narragansett Bay. In 1987, Rhode Island named the quahog its official state shell. American Indians used quahog shells to make wampum beads, which served as money.

RHODE ISLAND

Wallum Lake

Pascoag

CHEPACHET RIVER

BLACKSTONE RIVER

Woonsocket

Chepachet

Pawtucket

Providence

Jerimoth Hill

Scituate Reservoir

Foster

Cranston

PROVIDENCE RIVER

PAWTUXET RIVER

West Warwick

Warwick

MOUNT HOPE BAY

Flat River Reservoir

Tiverton

NARRAGANSETT BAY

WOOD RIVER

SAKONNET RIVER

Portsmouth

Newport

Fort Adams State Park

Ashaway

GREAT SWAMP

INDIAN CEDAR SWAMP

Worden Pond

RHODE ISLAND SOUND

Royal Indian Burial Ground

Point Judith Pond

Charlestown

N

BLOCK ISLAND SOUND

W

E

Block Island National Wildlife Refuge

S

BLOCK ISLAND

ATLANTIC OCEAN

The Ocean State

No matter where you are in Rhode Island, you are never far from the water. It is easy to see why Rhode Island has been nicknamed the Ocean State. Rhode Island is the smallest of the fifty states. It is only 48 miles (77 kilometers) from north to south and 37 miles (60 km) from east to west. A person can drive across the entire state in less than an hour. The state is divided into five counties. Rhode Island's land area spans 1,034 square miles (2,678 square kilometers). About 425 Rhode Islands could fit inside the largest U.S. state, Alaska. Because of its small size, the state is also called Little Rhody.

Size is not what defines Rhode Island, however. Rhode Island has played a big role in American history. It is the birthplace of religious freedom in what is now the United States. In 1776, Rhode Island was the first of the original thirteen colonies to declare independence from Great Britain.

America's factory system also traces its roots to Rhode Island. The country's first water-powered cotton mill was built here in the late eighteenth century. A mill is a factory that processes a raw material, such as cotton, paper, or steel. The Rhode Island mill introduced the United States to the Industrial Revolution. During this era,

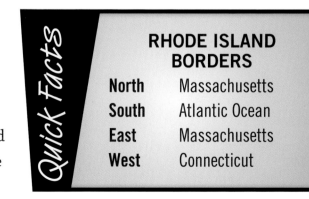

Quick Facts

RHODE ISLAND BORDERS

North	Massachusetts
South	Atlantic Ocean
East	Massachusetts
West	Connecticut

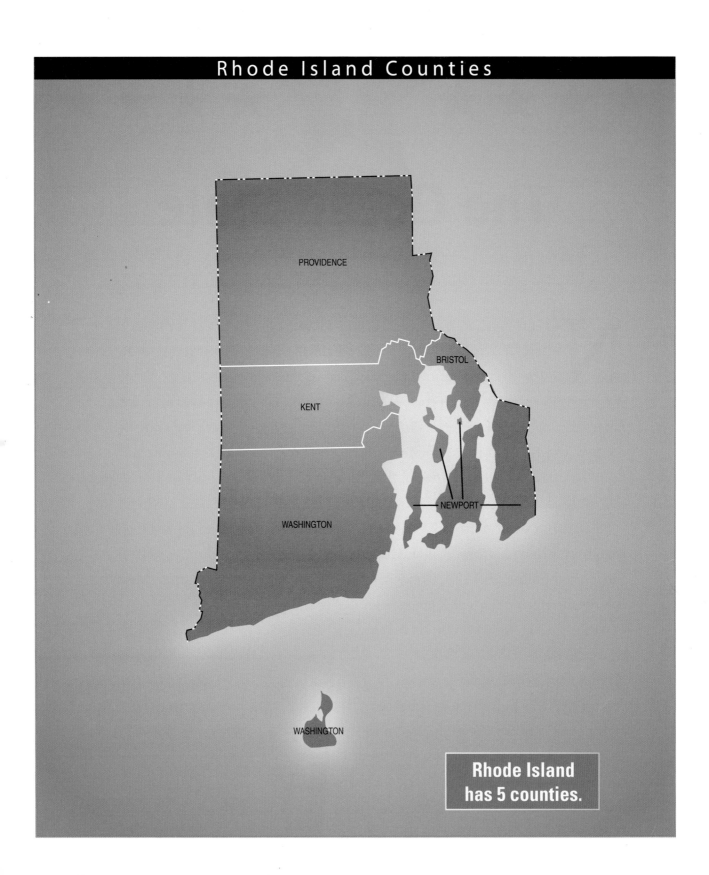

PROVIDENCE

BRISTOL

KENT

NEWPORT

WASHINGTON

WASHINGTON

**Rhode Island
has 5 counties.**

Narragansett Bay is an inlet of the Atlantic Ocean that extends almost 28 miles (45 km) into the state of Rhode Island.

manufacturing shifted from making goods using hand tools in homes or small shops to large-scale production in factories.

Just as interesting as Rhode Island's rich history is its impressive geography. Sounds, bays, inlets, and the Atlantic Ocean border Rhode Island. The jagged shores along Narragansett Bay and the state's thirty-plus islands form a coastline of more than 400 miles (640 km).

Rhode Island is one of six states that make up the northeastern region of the United States known as New England. The others are Connecticut, Maine, Massachusetts, New Hampshire, and Vermont. From its historic landmarks to its scenic shores, the Ocean State is filled with many exciting attractions for residents and visitors alike.

Shaping the State

Most of Rhode Island's natural features are a result of the movement of large sheets of ice called glaciers. Thousands of years ago, huge glaciers slowly expanded their reach south from the land now known as Canada and covered the region that includes Rhode Island and much of the northeastern United States. As they moved, the glaciers cut into the solid rock that lay beneath Earth's loose surface material. They also helped shape hills, carrying sand, clay, and rocks in the process.

With time, the glaciers began to melt and retreat back toward the north. The melting ice formed rivers. Water from the rushing rivers then washed gravel, sand, and other material onto the surrounding plains. It pushed up rocky cliffs and carved out lakes and ponds. The rushing water also created channels leading to the ocean. Natural changes to the land are responsible for many of Rhode Island's inland bodies of water. But some of the state's water bodies are human-made lakes, or reservoirs. Altogether, there are more than three hundred reservoirs, ponds, and natural freshwater lakes in Rhode Island. The movement of glaciers formed Rhode Island's two land regions. They are the Coastal Lowlands and the Eastern New England Upland.

Castle Hill Lighthouse, built in 1890, overlooks Narragansett Bay.

The Coastal Lowlands

The flat Coastal Lowlands cover much of Rhode Island. Most of the state's major cities and tourist attractions are located in this area. The lowlands include the eastern section of the state and all of its islands. The Coastal Lowlands region is made up mostly of sandy beaches, saltwater ponds, marshes, and lagoons. The state's lowest point is at sea level in the lowlands.

Narragansett Bay is a stretch of water that extends north from the Atlantic Ocean. It practically cuts the state in two. Rocky cliffs cover most of the bay's shores. Narragansett Bay is connected to other smaller bays, such as Greenwich Bay and Mount Hope Bay, and to many rivers, including the Providence River. East of the bay, the hills are rounded and wooded. To the west of the bay, the area has denser forests. Farther west, the ground gradually increases in elevation.

Providence is Rhode Island's capital. It is located on the mainland near the Providence River. Other towns and cities on the mainland in the coastal lowlands include Warwick, Cranston, Woonsocket, Charlestown, and Westerly.

Quick Facts

MOHEGAN BLUFFS

Large clay cliffs on Block Island called the Mohegan Bluffs offer spectacular views of the Atlantic Ocean. The Mohegan Bluffs tower 185 feet (56 meters) high. Glaciers shaped the cliffs thousands of years ago. Over time, the ocean has eroded, or worn away, the cliffs. As a result, Block Island's Southeast Lighthouse was moved back from the coast in 1993.

Newport, located on Aquidneck Island, was founded in 1639.

In and around Narragansett Bay are several islands. Some of these islands are home to towns and cities. Aquidneck Island, the largest island, includes Newport, Portsmouth, and Middletown. Newport is one of Rhode Island's most famous cities. A popular tourist destination, Newport has played a big role in the state's history.

All of the state's islands are located in or border Narragansett Bay except for Block Island. This popular vacation spot is the state's southernmost point. It is located in the Atlantic Ocean, about 12 miles (19 km) from the Rhode Island coast. The small island, which is only 7 miles (11 km) long and 3 miles (5 km) wide, is not connected to the mainland by any bridges or tunnels. The only way to get there is by plane or boat. Ferries carry visitors to Block Island. Nature trails, historic buildings, lighthouses, and other tourist attractions are found on the island. Bicyclists and hikers enjoy its scenic beauty. It is also home to about eight hundred year-round residents. The residents of Block Island have their own town government, school system, and other public services.

Boaters take an evening sail by the Newport Bridge, which spans Narragansett Bay.

The Eastern New England Upland

The Eastern New England Upland, which extends from Connecticut to Maine, stretches through the northern and western regions of Rhode Island. It covers about one-third of the state's total area. Rolling hills, narrow valleys, wooded areas, ponds, lakes, and reservoirs mark this scenic region, which is also called the Western Rocky Upland. The area has higher elevations than the Coastal Lowlands. In the far western edge of the state—near the Connecticut border—is Jerimoth Hill. At 812 feet (247 m) above sea level, Jerimoth Hill is the highest point in Rhode Island.

The western portion of the state is dotted with small towns and cities, rivers, reservoirs, and lakes. Much of the land is ideal for growing hay, corn, and potatoes. The wooded areas in the region are filled with a variety of trees, including oak, maple, hickory, birch, pine, spruce, cedar, and hemlock. Parts of

SCITUATE RESERVOIR

Scituate Reservoir is the largest reservoir in Rhode Island. In the 1920s, a dam, built on a section of the Pawtuxet River, created the artificial lake. Located in north-central Rhode Island, Scituate Reservoir provides water to most of the state.

Rhode Island's Upland are perfect for those who enjoy outdoor activities such as hiking, canoeing, fishing, and horseback riding.

Climate

Rhode Island's climate tends to be milder than that of its New England neighbors. This means that Rhode Island—mostly the southern, southeastern, and coastal areas—usually has warmer winter temperatures. The higher temperatures are a result of the winds blowing in from the Atlantic Ocean and Narragansett Bay. The northern and northwestern sections of Rhode Island tend to have cooler year-round temperatures than southern and coastal Rhode Island. In the summer, the coast and the southern portions of the state are slightly warmer than the northern sections.

In general, the coldest months in the state are January and February. During January, Rhode Islanders can expect an average temperature of about 29 degrees Fahrenheit (–2 degrees Celsius). The lowest temperature in the state occurred on February 5, 1996, when the city of Greene recorded a frigid –25 °F (–32 °C).

Swimmers and sunbathers enjoy a hot summer day at a Newport beach.

The warmest months in Rhode Island are July and August. The average July temperature is 73 °F (23 °C). The heat became pretty intense for residents of Providence on August 2, 1975, when the temperature climbed to a record-breaking 104 °F (40 °C).

Precipitation is the amount of water that falls as rain, snow, or other moisture. Rhode Island's average precipitation is about 47 inches (119 centimeters) per year, though the southwestern part tends to be wetter than the rest of the state. Annual snowfall in the state amounts to about 31 inches (79 cm).

Hurricanes and floods have been the fiercest weather events that Rhode Islanders living in coastal areas have had to deal with over the years. Hurricanes usually

Quick Facts

THE HURRICANE OF 1938

On September 21, 1938, a powerful hurricane slammed into New England, hitting Rhode Island especially hard. A huge wave of water called a storm surge crashed into the state. Entire communities were wiped out. The hurricane killed 262 people in Rhode Island.

strike in late summer and early fall. Strong hurricane winds can damage or destroy homes and other buildings. The heavy rains and strong, tall waves from hurricanes often cause flooding and structural damage to buildings. Throughout Rhode Island's history, hurricanes have caused millions of dollars of damage.

Wildlife

Rhode Island hosts a wide variety of plants and animals. More than 60 percent of the state is forested. Around sixty different species, or types, of trees thrive in Rhode Island. They include ashes, hickories, elms, maples, poplars, beeches, willows, birches, and Atlantic white cedars. In the warm-weather months, inland fields are often dotted with colorful wildflowers, such as goldenrod, asters, violets, and lilies. Flowering plants also populate the state's wooded areas. Among these are mountain laurels, wild roses, dogwoods, azaleas, blue gentians, orchids, irises, and rhododendrons.

Many wild mammals roam Rhode Island's wooded areas as well. They include white-tailed deer, skunks, rabbits, raccoons, squirrels, moles, foxes, and woodchucks. Beavers, muskrats, otters, and mink can be spotted swimming in the state's ponds, rivers, and lakes. Other inhabitants of these freshwater areas include fish such as bass, perch, pike, trout, and pickerel.

The salty coastal waters are home to swordfish, striped bass, flounder, sharks, tuna, mackerel, jellyfish, bluefish, cod, and butterfish. Shellfish also thrive, particularly lobsters, soft-shell crabs, oysters, scallops,

A variety of wildflowers grow in Rhode Island's fields, forests, and coastal areas.

Harbor seals rest on rocks on Block Island. They feed on fish, shellfish, and squid.

mussels, and clams. During winter months, harbor seals can be found lounging on Block Island's rocks and beaches.

More than four hundred species of birds have been spotted in the state. Inhabiting Rhode Island's wooded areas are robins, owls, blue jays, flickers, sparrows, and catbirds. Looking for meals of fish and shellfish along the coast are seagulls, terns, osprey, and loons. Geese and ducks live near the state's waterways. Rhode Island also has some game birds, which are hunted during specific times of the year. These birds include pheasants, quails, and partridges.

Wildlife at Risk

Rhode Island has gone to great lengths to protect its wildlife. However, a rise in pollution over the years has put some types of wildlife in the state in danger of disappearing completely from their ranges. The U.S. government keeps a list of endangered and threatened species. When a type of animal or plant is endangered, it is at risk of dying out in its range or a large area of its range. A threatened species is at risk of becoming endangered. Rhode Island has several endangered species, including the roseate tern, the American burying beetle, and three types of sea turtles.

The Block Island National Wildlife Refuge supports the endangered American burying beetle. It has the only known population of the species east of the Mississippi River.

Plants & Animals

Muskrat

This large rodent, covered with brownish fur, can grow more than 14 inches (36 cm) long. Muskrats make their homes around Rhode Island's numerous ponds, lakes, and rivers by piecing together piles of twigs, branches, leaves, and other plant material. A muskrat's flattened tail—which acts like a boat's rudder—and its partially webbed back feet help the animal swim.

White-Tailed Deer

These graceful, swift animals have red-brown fur in the summer that changes to a grayish brown during the winter months. An adult male deer, or buck, can weigh nearly 300 pounds (140 kilograms). Young white-tailed deer, or fawns, have reddish brown fur with white spots to help camouflage them. As a fawn gets older, its spots disappear.

Blue Jay

People recognize this woodland bird, which is part of the crow family, by its bright blue, black, and white color and the pointy crest at the top of its head. Blue jays may be as long as 12 inches (30 cm). They eat mostly insects, nuts, and seeds.

Bluefish

Bluefish are a common sight along Rhode Island's Atlantic coastline, particularly in the spring when they prey on other fish moving toward the shore to breed. Fishing for bluefish and their young, known as snappers, is a popular sport in Rhode Island. The largest bluefish caught on record weighed in at more than 25 pounds (11 kg). But bluefish typically weigh between 5 pounds and 15 pounds (2 kg and 7 kg).

Goldenrod

Goldenrod is a wildflower that graces Rhode Island's meadows, woods, and hills in autumn. It has a wandlike stem with clusters of brilliant yellow-colored flowers. The plant can grow to a height of 4 feet (1 m).

Paper Birch

Sometimes called white birches or canoe birches, paper birch trees are found mainly in Rhode Island's northern wooded areas. The trees have sheets of bark that peel off in layers and remind people of sheets of paper. In the past, American Indians used the sturdy but flexible bark of these tall trees to build canoes.

From the Beginning

Many historians and scientists estimate that the first humans arrived in the region that now includes Rhode Island around 8000 BCE. These people were the ancestors of present-day American Indians. They were mainly hunters and gatherers who looked for food in the area's thick forests and coastal waters. These early people lived in small communities and made tools out of stone. Eventually, they began growing crops such as corn, beans, squash, cucumbers, tobacco, and pumpkins.

In the early seventeenth century, about ten thousand American Indians lived in the area. They made up five main tribes: the Nipmuc, Niantic, Wampanoag, Narragansett, and Pequot. All of these groups were a part of the Algonquians, a large collection of northeastern tribes that shared customs and related languages.

Most of the American Indians living in the region that now includes Rhode Island settled in villages near water. Being close to water gave them easy access to sources of food and trade. Some lived in wigwams, round-roofed structures with frames made of wooden poles. The frames were covered with deer hide, tree bark, or reeds that were stitched together. Others lived in long, narrow homes called longhouses.

Except for occasional battles between the Narragansett (the largest and most powerful group in the region) and the Wampanoag (who inhabited the

English settler Roger Williams, who founded the colony of Rhode Island, met Narragansett Indians and learned their language in the winter of 1635–1636.

far eastern parts), the tribes managed to live together peacefully. They also had a system of government in which village leaders who functioned as judges decided legal and spiritual disputes.

The First European Settlers

In the early 1500s, Portuguese explorers may have spotted the land now known as Rhode Island as they sailed by. However, the first known European to explore the area was an Italian sailor named Giovanni da Verrazzano. Sailing for France in 1524, Verrazzano landed near present-day Block Island. Nearly a hundred years later, Dutch sea captain Adriaen Block became the next European to sail by the area, in 1614. Block Island is named after him.

Giovanni da Verrazzano was the first European to explore Narragansett Bay and New York harbor.

In 1630, about one thousand members of a religious group known as the Puritans left England to start a colony north of present-day Rhode Island. A colony is land settled and governed by another country. The Puritans had left their native country because they disagreed with the Church of England. They believed in firm obedience to church laws, which were strictly enforced by their

Quick Facts

HOW DID RHODE ISLAND GET ITS NAME?
The name *Rhode Island* was first used in the mid-1600s. No one knows for sure the origin of the name. Some people credit Italian explorer Giovanni da Verrazzano, who thought Block Island, part of today's Rhode Island, resembled the Greek island of Rhodes. Others credit Dutch navigator Adriaen Block, who described the state's largest island, Aquidneck Island, which has reddish soil, as *Roodt Eylandt*—"red island" in Dutch.

RHODE ISLAND'S FIRST EUROPEAN SETTLER

In 1623, an English minister named William Blackstone, displeased with the Church of England, joined an expedition sailing to present-day Massachusetts. Then, in 1635, Blackstone became the first European to settle in the area that is now Rhode Island. The Blackstone River in northeastern Rhode Island is named after him.

colony's governor, John Winthrop. Their settlement, called the Massachusetts Bay Colony, included what is today Boston and Salem.

Rhode Island's Founder: Roger Williams

In 1631, Roger Williams, an English preacher, arrived in Boston. Unlike the other Puritans of Massachusetts Bay, Williams believed in complete religious freedom. He believed that individuals should be free to worship God however they desire and that the laws of a church and of government should be separate. In addition, Williams, who had made friends with American Indians and respected their way of life, thought white settlers should treat them fairly and pay them for land taken by settlers.

Williams's beliefs conflicted with those of the Puritan leaders of the Massachusetts Bay Colony and officials arrested him on several occasions. By 1635, they had banished him from the colony. Before Williams could be sent back to England, he fled south. Within a few days, he arrived at the eastern side of Narragansett Bay, where the Wampanoag and their leader, Massasoit, welcomed him. He also met Narragansett Indians.

A statue of the founder of Rhode Island stands in Providence's Roger Williams Park.

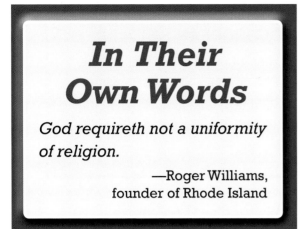
Other white settlers seeking religious freedom soon joined Williams. In June 1636, he purchased land from Massasoit and two Narragansett leaders, Canonicus and Miantonomo. The land was located at the northern tip of Narragansett Bay. There, Williams created the first permanent settlement in what is now Rhode Island. He named it Providence. He felt that God's providence, or "watchful eye," had kept him safe and guided him on his trip from Boston. Word about Williams's new colony and its religious freedom spread throughout Massachusetts Bay. Other settlements soon sprang up in the area that now includes present-day Portsmouth, Newport, and Warwick.

Quick Facts

ANNE HUTCHINSON

In 1634, Anne Hutchinson (1591–1643) moved with her family from England to the Massachusetts Bay Colony in search of religious freedom. She challenged the religious views of Puritan leaders with her preaching. Puritan officials believed that women should not be able to preach. Like Roger Williams, Hutchinson was banned from the colony. With the help of Williams, she and her followers founded present-day Portsmouth in Rhode Island in 1638. (Other Hutchinson followers headed south and founded Newport in 1639.) After her husband's death, Hutchinson moved to Long Island in New York. She was killed in 1643 during a fight with American Indians.

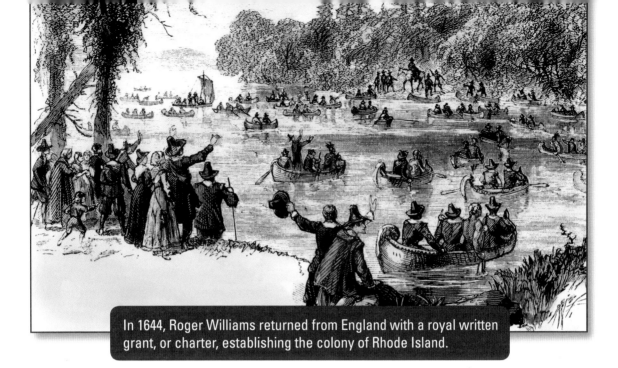

In 1644, Roger Williams returned from England with a royal written grant, or charter, establishing the colony of Rhode Island.

The Charters

In 1644, the English Parliament granted Williams a written assurance of rights called a charter. The charter recognized the four settlements of Providence, Portsmouth, Newport, and Warwick as the colony of Providence Plantations. In 1647, the four settlements were officially united. Representatives from each settlement met at Portsmouth. They set up a system of government that included a representative assembly and a president. It was decided that the settlements' male inhabitants would elect the president.

By the 1650s, Roger Williams's vision of religious freedom and tolerance for all made Rhode Island a popular place for people of different faiths. In 1663, King Charles II of England granted the four settlements a new royal charter. The charter gave the colony the name Rhode Island and Providence Plantations. The charter provided the new colony with a large amount of self-government— more than any of the other English colonies in North America, including Connecticut, Massachusetts Bay, and Virginia. The charter also authorized the colony to continue Roger Williams's "lively experiment" of freedom of religion for all.

Religious freedom in the colony continued to grow. People of all faiths were welcome. In Providence, in 1638, Williams established the first Baptist church in what is now the United States. Another group of Christians called Quakers built a meetinghouse on Aquidneck Island in 1657. People of Jewish faith began settling in Rhode Island in the 1650s, and their numbers continued to grow. In 1763, the Touro Synagogue opened in Newport. It is the oldest Jewish house of worship in the United States, and it is now a national historic site.

King Philip's War

For nearly forty years after Roger Williams founded Providence, Rhode Island's colonists had peaceful relations with the area's American Indians. That is partly because Williams believed that, as the first inhabitants of the area, American Indians were the rightful owners of the land and should be paid for losing it. In other colonies, however, settlers were taking land from American Indians without payment. As a result, some tribes began to fight against the colonists.

In 1675, Metacomet, a Wampanoag leader whom the settlers called King Philip, began attacking English settlements. He convinced other groups in the region—the Nipmuc, Mohegan, and Podunk—to join the Wampanoag in protecting their lands.

At first, King Philip targeted only colonial settlements in Massachusetts Bay. That changed, however, when militias—groups of trained fighters—from Connecticut and Massachusetts Bay attacked and defeated a group of American Indian warriors near a southern Rhode Island town now called Kingston. The battle became known as the Great Swamp Fight. But the colonial militias did not stop there. They continued to raid and burn surrounding American Indian villages. Within a few days, the colonists had killed more than a thousand American Indian men, women, and children.

The 1675–1676 conflict between American Indians and white settlers in southern New England was called King Philip's War.

King Philip and his allies began attacking settlements in Rhode Island as well as Massachusetts Bay. They set Providence on fire. Settlers from the town and neighboring areas were forced to flee to the colony's offshore islands. In 1676, King Philip was killed in a battle near present-day Bristol, Rhode Island. The series of battles between American Indians and English colonists became known as King Philip's War.

The Narragansett, Wampanoag, Nipmuc, Mohegan, and Podunk groups were practically wiped out as a result of the war. Several hundred of King Philip's warriors were also captured and sold into slavery in other countries. The relationships between the Rhode Island colonists and the region's American Indians were never quite the same again. The American Indians who remained did not have much power against the white settlers. Some moved away while others gave up their traditional lifestyles to fit in with the colonists.

The Triangle Trade

The early 1700s marked the beginning of a period of great prosperity for Rhode Island. The colony's population grew from just 7,000 people in 1710 to 40,000

REDWOOD LIBRARY AND ATHENAEUM

Established in Newport in 1747, the Redwood Library and Athenaeum is the first library in Rhode Island and the oldest lending library in the United States. In a lending library, members pay fees to access materials. One of Redwood's most famous librarians, Ezra Stiles (1727–1795), helped found Brown University in Providence. He later became the president of Yale University in New Haven, Connecticut.

in 1755. Farming and whaling were very profitable businesses. Candles and other products were made from whale oil. Sea trading was also important to the colony's economy. In fact, the colony's merchants sold and traded everything from wood, salt, cider, dairy products, and molasses to horses, fish, and preserved meats. Rhode Island's coasts made it easy for ships to come in and sail out carrying a wide variety of goods. Within a short period of time, Newport and Providence emerged as bustling ports in colonial America.

By the mid-1700s, Newport was one of the busiest ports in the American colonies.

Rhode Island merchants prospered from the slave trade. In fact, they controlled between 60 and 90 percent of the American trade in African slaves. Rhode Island's prosperity during this period depended on its trade relationship with the West Indies called the Triangle Trade. The West Indies is a group of islands in the Caribbean Sea. The three points in the Triangle Trade were Rhode Island, Africa, and the West Indies.

Rhode Island merchants would send the alcoholic beverage called rum to Africa. The rum had been made in Rhode Island with molasses from the West Indies. Once the rum arrived in Africa, it was exchanged for African slaves. The slaves—who were needed to work on the sugar plantations in the West Indies— were shipped to the West Indies and traded for molasses. The molasses was then sent to Rhode Island and turned into additional rum. The cycle repeated over and over, bringing great profit to Rhode Island traders.

Slave ships were dirty and crowded. Many slaves died from the horrible conditions. Some slaves from Africa ended up working in Rhode Island. By 1774, slaves made up more than 6 percent of Rhode Island's population. In 1784, Rhode Island passed a law that freed the children of slaves. The international slave trade, however, continued into the 1800s.

Quick Facts

NEWPORT'S FURNITURE MAKERS

In the mid-1700s, Newport was a major furniture-making center. Two of colonial America's best-known furniture makers—the Townsend and Goddard families—lived and worked in Easton's Point, a Quaker neighborhood in Newport. Many of their best-known pieces were made from mahogany wood imported from the West Indies.

Today, Newport furniture from the eighteenth century is very valuable. Many world-class museums include Townsend-Goddard pieces in their collections. In 1989, a mahogany Goddard desk and bookcase made in the 1760s sold for $12.1 million. It was the highest price ever paid for a piece of furniture.

MAKING A POMANDER BALL

Colonial homes often used pomander balls as natural air fresheners. They sometimes masked odors that came from cooking in an open fireplace. These air fresheners are still popular today as holiday decorations or as gifts.

WHAT YOU NEED

Paper towels

Roll of masking tape, about $^1/_4$ inch (0.5 cm) wide

Medium-sized orange

Nail or screw

20 to 30 whole cloves

1 tablespoon (15 grams) ground cinnamon

1 tablespoon (15 g) ground nutmeg

1 tablespoon (15 g) ground allspice

Tissue paper

3 feet (1 m) of narrow ribbon, about $^1/_2$ inch (1 cm) wide

Spread several paper towels on your work surface. Wrap one piece of tape around the orange to divide it in half. Wrap another piece of tape around the orange to divide it in half the other way.

With the help of an adult, use the nail or screw to make about twenty holes in the skin of the orange. Poke holes around the orange, avoiding the tape.

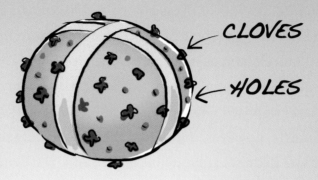

Push the cloves into the orange, but do not put the cloves into the holes you just made. You can use the nail or screw to make new small holes for the cloves. Be sure not to put any cloves through the tape.

Remove the tape. Then mix the cinnamon, nutmeg, and allspice together on a piece of paper towel. Roll the orange around in the spices. You can push some of the spices into the first holes you made with the nail.

Carefully wrap the orange in tissue paper. Store the orange in a cool, dark, and dry place for about three weeks. It will shrink and harden. Have an adult help you pick the right place. If the spot is not dry and dark, the orange can spoil. Also, be sure the orange is out of the reach of pets.

Once the orange has dried out, remove the tissue paper. Wrap the ribbon around the orange, following the path you used for the masking tape. Ask an adult for help if you need extra hands to tie the ribbon. Make a double knot at the top of the orange. Make a loop with the ends of the ribbon, and tie the loop with a bow. The loop can be used to hang the pomander ball. Hang the ball to freshen a room, or give it as a pleasant-smelling gift.

Acts of Rebellion

Around the time that Rhode Island was experiencing its economic prosperity, Great Britain was involved in a series of wars with France for control over much of North America. The last of these struggles was known as the French and Indian War (1754–1763). Great Britain defeated France in the conflict, gaining almost all of France's land east of the Mississippi River. During the struggle, Great Britain expected its colonies to provide troops, and even after the fighting was over, Britain imposed fees and taxes on the colonists to help pay for the war.

Many colonists, however, opposed the new British taxes. They said repaying the war debt was Britain's responsibility. In 1764, the British Parliament dealt the colonists a heavy blow. It passed the Sugar Act. This law required colonists to pay a tax on imported goods such as molasses, sugar, and wine. These taxes angered the colonists, especially those who earned their living from the Triangle Trade. The next year, the British Parliament passed the Stamp Act, which taxed paper items—from legal documents to playing cards—in the colonies. The colonists were angered even further.

In protest and to avoid paying taxes, some merchants smuggled molasses, sugar, and other taxable goods into the colony. The colonists' general unrest eventually led to violence. In 1769, colonists burned the British ship *Liberty* in Newport's waters. Then, on June 10, 1772, a group of Providence merchants led by John Brown lured a British customs ship called the *Gaspee* into Narragansett Bay and set it on fire. A customs ship was responsible for

In 1772, angry Rhode Island colonists burned the ship *Gaspee* in Narragansett Bay to protest British taxation.

enforcing British taxes on imported goods. The *Gaspee*'s commander was shot and wounded during the colonists' attack. These events in Rhode Island marked the first acts of colonial rebellion against Great Britain.

The American Revolution

Less than three years after the burning of the *Gaspee*, in the spring of 1775, colonists in Massachusetts Bay fought British troops at Lexington and Concord. It was the beginning of the American Revolution. Rhode Island immediately sent troops to help its colonial neighbor fight the British. In June, George Washington was appointed the leader of an army—called the Continental Army—that would bring together soldiers from all of the thirteen colonies.

Washington was appointed by the Second Continental Congress, which was meeting in Philadelphia, Pennsylvania, and included representatives, or delegates, from the thirteen colonies. Rhode Island's delegates urged the formation of an American fleet, and the Continental Navy was established in October 1775. Stephen and Esek Hopkins, two brothers from Rhode Island, helped create the Continental Navy. Esek Hopkins became its first commander in chief.

Like the rest of the colonies, Rhode Island wanted to be free of British rule. On May 4, 1776, Rhode Island became the first New England colony to declare independence from Great Britain. Two months later, on July 4, 1776, delegates from all thirteen colonies, at the Continental Congress, approved the Declaration of Independence, stating that "these United Colonies are, and of Right ought to be, Free and Independent States." There were several more years of war ahead, however.

The American Revolution included many battles throughout the colonies, and Rhode Island soldiers took part in the fighting. Residents in the colony who supported independence also provided supplies, money, and food for the troops. In August 1778, one of the largest land battles of the American Revolution took place near Newport. It became known as the Battle of Rhode Island. General Nathanael Greene, a Rhode Islander, led American troops during the battle. With the help of forces from France, which was aiding the colonists during the

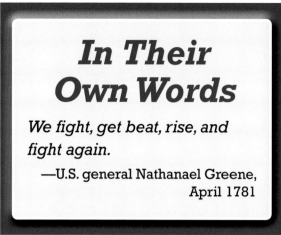
American Revolution, the Continental Army tried to win back Newport from British troops, but the Americans were forced to retreat.

Also fighting in the Battle of Rhode Island was a group of soldiers called the Black Regiment of Rhode Island. They formed the first African-American army unit. The soldiers were made up of more than 120 black men, including about 100 enslaved Africans.

Later in the war, Greene played a key role in the final British defeat. Under his leadership, American troops in the South forced a British army led by General Cornwallis to retreat to Yorktown, Virginia, in 1781. There, George Washington and his troops, supported by French forces, trapped and attacked Cornwallis's army. The British were forced to surrender.

In 1783, the former thirteen colonies—now the United States of America— signed a peace agreement with Great Britain called the Treaty of Paris, in which Britain officially accepted American independence. In 1787, the U.S. Constitution was drafted at a convention in Philadelphia. The document outlined how the U.S. government would operate and what powers it would have. Each state had to ratify (approve) the Constitution.

Rhode Islanders were concerned about giving up too much power to the federal government, however. They refused to ratify the Constitution until it included additional rights that would protect individual liberties and limit federal authority. Finally, the U.S. Congress approved the first ten amendments to the Constitution, called the Bill of Rights. On May 29, 1790, Rhode Island approved the U.S. Constitution. It was the last of the original thirteen colonies to do so.

The Industrial Revolution Begins

In the late 1700s and into the 1800s, Rhode Island's economy prospered. With the beginning of the Industrial Revolution, manufacturing became a huge

Slater Mill was the birthplace of the U.S. textile industry.
Today, the historic building in Pawtucket is open to the public.

industry in the state. A rich and powerful Providence merchant named
Moses Brown had been operating a mill that spun cotton in Pawtucket on the
Blackstone River. Brown had visited Great Britain and witnessed how British
cotton mills used water-powered machines to spin cotton into thread. These
machines allowed the British mills to produce goods faster and cheaper. Brown
wished he knew how to build and run such machines, but British mill owners,
not wanting competition from other countries, guarded their operations. In
fact, anyone who worked in a water-powered cotton mill in Great Britain was
forbidden to leave the country.

However, one mill worker did manage to slip out undetected. Samuel Slater
disguised himself as a farmer, boarded a ship, and ended up in Pawtucket in
1790. Slater worked with Brown to re-create a water-powered mill similar to
those in Great Britain. The rolling Blackstone River was the perfect source for
setting a gigantic waterwheel in motion. In 1793, Slater created the first water-
powered cotton mill in the United States.

Within a few years, other mills sprang up along Rhode Island's many rivers.
Textiles (cloth) became a leading industry for the state. The use of water to power
mills was also applied to other industries. David Wilkinson, another Pawtucket

businessman, developed a water-powered mill to manufacture metal tools and equipment. Rhode Island's economy shifted from farming and sea trading to manufacturing.

The state also became famous for its jewelry and silverware industries. In 1794, two brothers, Nehemiah and Seril Dodge, started making costume jewelry in Providence. They found a way to cover cheaper metals with better-looking and more expensive metals. With this innovation, Rhode Island entered the jewelry industry. By 1824, Providence had become the jewelry-making capital of North America.

In the 1830s, silversmith Jabez Gorham began manufacturing sterling silver. It is a pure silver melted with another metal, often copper, to make it stronger. At first, Jabez Gorham made spoons, thimbles, and jewelry. In time, under the direction of his son, John, the Gorham Manufacturing Company grew into the largest sterling silver manufacturer in the world. Many U.S. presidents have served their guests using Gorham silverware.

From the 1840s through the 1850s, railroad lines began to cross through Rhode Island. The railroads helped connect Rhode Island to other states, making it easier and cheaper for Rhode Island factories to ship their products around the country. Manufacturing became even more profitable.

As word of the state's economic prosperity spread, it began to attract people from other countries seeking better opportunities. Soon, a steady stream of immigrants made their way into the state. Rhode Island's population skyrocketed from just under 70,000 in 1800 to almost 148,000 in 1850.

The Dorr Rebellion

Newcomers to Rhode Island found they had little voice in the state's government. The royal charter that King Charles II of England had granted Rhode Island's colonists in 1663 was still in effect. According to the charter, only male property owners and their oldest sons could vote. In 1840, that meant a large part of the state's adult population could not participate in state government. Those who were permitted to vote lived mainly in the state's rural areas. People who worked in the crowded cities—including the newly arrived immigrants who could not afford to buy land—were left underrepresented in decisions about the state government.

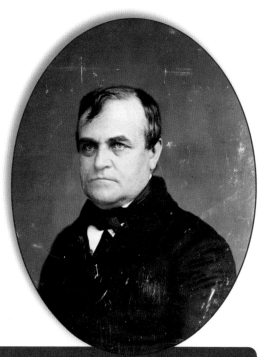

Thomas Dorr began a rebellion to change Rhode Island's voting rights in 1841.

In 1841, a Providence attorney named Thomas Dorr felt something had to be done. He tried to reform, or change, the state's outdated charter. The movement became known as the Dorr Rebellion. Dorr and his supporters formed the People's Party. They drafted a new constitution that extended voting rights to all adult males who lived within the state. Members of the party then held their own statewide election and elected Dorr as their governor in 1842. Dorr was arrested, convicted of treason—betraying his country—and sentenced to life in prison. He was released after serving only a year. The Dorr Rebellion led to a revised state constitution in 1843. The change allowed males, including African Americans, born in the United States to vote without owning property.

The Civil War

Not long after Abraham Lincoln was elected the sixteenth U.S. president in 1860, the Civil War (1861–1865) broke out. This conflict bitterly divided Northern and Southern states. People in those states disagreed on slavery

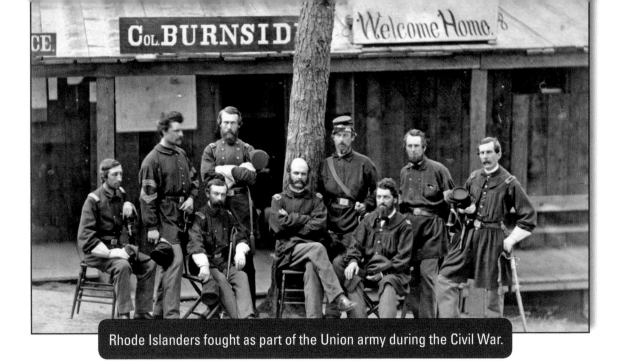

Rhode Islanders fought as part of the Union army during the Civil War.

and other issues. Most Northerners opposed slavery. Most Southerners believed they had the right to own slaves.

Southern states feared Lincoln's election would lead to restrictions on or even the abolition of slavery. By late 1860 and early 1861, eleven Southern states decided to secede, or break away, from the Union (another name for the United States at the time). They formed a new government of their own called the Confederate States of America. Lincoln raised a large army and went to war to bring the Confederate states back into the Union and keep all the states united as a single country.

Rhode Island manufacturers had been buying a great deal of cotton from Southern states to keep their textile mills running. As a result, some Rhode Islanders did not want to fight against the Confederacy. Eventually, though, Rhode Island contributed more than 24,000 troops to the Union army. The state's factories and farms provided supplies and food for Union troops.

After years of fighting and the loss of hundreds of thousands of lives, the South surrendered to the North in 1865. The Union victory meant the United States would remain one nation. After the Civil War ended, the Thirteenth Amendment to the U.S. Constitution was adopted, outlawing slavery throughout the United States.

The Gilded Age

Rhode Island's economy and population continued to grow after the Civil War. The state's textile mills produced thread, yarn, cotton shirts, and other goods. These were then shipped to countries all over the world. Rhode Island's jewelry and metal-products industries were also flourishing. Industries in other parts of the United States were prospering as well.

This economic prosperity set the stage for a period in the late 1800s known as the Gilded Age, or Golden Age. During this time, many of the country's richest families—the Astor, Vanderbilt, Morgan, and Belmont families—chose to spend summers in Newport. Members of these elite families, most of them based in New York, were famous business leaders who made huge fortunes in manufacturing, transportation, and banking. They built stunning seaside mansions in Newport. Many of the mansions are located on Newport's Bellevue Avenue and have been designated National Historic Landmarks.

THE BREAKERS

A popular tourist attraction in Newport is a seventy-room summer "cottage" known as the Breakers. New York tycoon Cornelius Vanderbilt II built the Breakers, Newport's grandest mansion, in the 1890s. His family made its fortune in steamships and railroads. Thirty-three of the mansion's rooms were required for Vanderbilt's servants alone. The main rooms are filled with finely polished marble and alabaster, glistening crystal chandeliers, velvet draperies and cushions, and walls covered with gold leaf. The estate offers amazing views of the Atlantic Ocean.

Other mansions, such as Hammersmith Farm, built in 1887, have been turned into private residences. The wedding reception of Jacqueline Bouvier and John F. Kennedy was held at Hammersmith Farm in 1953. Jacqueline spent summers as a child in the twenty-eight-room Victorian mansion. During President Kennedy's time in office, Hammersmith Farm became known as the Summer White House due to his frequent visits.

The Twentieth Century

In the 1900s, more immigrants were drawn to Rhode Island's industrial success. They looked for work in the state's many factories. Most of the immigrants came from Italy, Ireland, Great Britain, Portugal, Russia, Poland, and French-speaking areas of Canada. Some of these groups had started immigrating even earlier. In Providence alone, the population soared from about 55,000 in 1865 to more than 175,000 in 1900. By 1925, Providence's population reached an all-time peak of 267,918.

The factories that provided goods and money for the state economy were not pleasant places to work. Factory workers put in long hours in buildings that were cold during the winter and hot during the summer. Some of the machinery was dangerous and workers often suffered injuries while on the job. Even young children went to work in factories and mills to help their families earn money. In the early 1900s, some reforms were made to try to protect workers from the most dangerous conditions. But the average working family still had a very difficult time making a living.

In 1914, World War I had begun in Europe. When the United States entered the war in 1917, Rhode Island provided supplies and troops to the American war effort. By the time the war ended in 1918, several of Rhode Island's industries were no longer as profitable. Many of the state's textile companies had moved their mills to southern states where laborers were willing to work for lower wages.

Things grew worse for the Ocean State—and for the rest of the country— during the Great Depression. The Great Depression began when the stock market

Narragansett Bay and Newport were centers of naval activity during World War II. In the decades after the war, submarines continued to use Narragansett Bay for training.

collapsed in 1929. Many people lost all of their money. Businesses closed down. Thousands of people were out of work. Rhode Island's once-thriving textile industry had practically disappeared. The federal government established some programs to help people find jobs and feed their families, but it was a very difficult time.

The economy began to improve during World War II (1939–1945). When the United States entered the war in 1941, American factories reopened. They began manufacturing goods for the war effort. Farm products were again needed to feed the troops. Rhode Island's factories made a huge contribution by producing ammunition, chemicals, machinery, electronics, and other war materials. U.S. troops used metal shelters called Quonset huts for storage, housing, and medical centers during the war. These huts were developed at the Quonset Point Naval Air Station in Rhode Island. About 92,000 Rhode Islanders served in the armed forces in World War II.

Once the war was over, Rhode Island faced difficult economic times again. Factories had stopped building war

Quick Facts

NAVAL TORPEDO STATION
During World War II, many Rhode Islanders went to work in the state's factories. Women helped produce about 17,000 torpedoes at the Naval Torpedo Station on Newport's Goat Island.

materials. The number of people without jobs became alarmingly high. To replace Rhode Island's declining textile industry, efforts were made to attract other types of businesses.

Over the next several decades, companies specializing in electronic equipment, plastics, machinery, chemicals, health care products, and toys began moving into the state. They provided jobs and helped to stimulate the economy. Numerous new roads and highways were also built to accommodate the growing state.

Rhode Island Today

In the twenty-first century, Rhode Island remains a popular vacation spot. But like the rest of the country, the state suffered difficult times after a severe nationwide economic recession began at the end of 2007. Many people lost their jobs, and several years later, Rhode Island still had one of the highest unemployment rates of any U.S. state.

The state is planning new business initiatives. Old factories in Providence's former jewelry district have been converted into grand buildings in the new Knowledge District. The focus is on bringing more jobs in health care and other "knowledge-based" industries to this district. Brown University recently opened a $45-million medical school here. Government officials hope such initiatives will help revitalize the state's economy.

Today's Providence is looking to attract new jobs in high-tech fields.

Important Dates

★ **8000 BCE** Ancestors of present-day American Indians inhabit the region.

★ **1524** Giovanni da Verrazzano becomes the first European known to reach Rhode Island.

★ **1614** Dutch sailor Adriaen Block arrives on the land now called Block Island.

★ **1636** Puritan leader Roger Williams establishes Providence, the first settlement in Rhode Island.

★ **1644** The English Parliament grants Roger Williams a charter that recognizes the four settlements of Providence, Portsmouth, Newport, and Warwick as the colony of Providence Plantations.

★ **1663** King Charles II of England grants Providence Plantations a new royal charter, allowing it more self-government and religious freedom.

★ **1675** American Indians and white settlers begin fighting King Philip's War.

★ **1763** Touro Synagogue, the oldest synagogue in the present-day United States, is built in Newport.

★ **1772** Colonists set fire to the British ship *Gaspee* in Narragansett Bay.

★ **1776** Rhode Island is the first colony to declare independence from Great Britain.

★ **1784** Rhode Island passes a law that frees the children of slaves.

★ **1790** Rhode Island becomes the thirteenth state.

★ **1793** Samuel Slater builds the first U.S. water-powered cotton-spinning mill, helping to launch the Industrial Revolution in the country.

★ **1841** Thomas Dorr begins a rebellion to change voting rights.

★ **1895** Construction is completed on the grand Breakers mansion in Newport.

★ **1969** The Newport Bridge connects Jamestown to Newport over Narragansett Bay.

★ **1990** Rhode Island celebrates two hundred years of statehood.

★ **2011** Brown University opens its new medical school in Providence's Knowledge District.

The People

Before the first Europeans arrived, American Indians inhabited the area that now includes Rhode Island. Many Europeans eventually came to the region looking for new land and religious freedom. Until the early 1800s, most of these new settlers made their living by farming, fishing, shipbuilding, and trading.

As new technologies developed, manufacturing became the center of Rhode Island's economy. Factories sprang up quickly in the state's major cities. With the increase in factories came the need for more people to work in them. Rhode Island became a magnet for European and other immigrants, attracting a steady stream of people from a wide variety of backgrounds and nationalities.

The Irish began immigrating to Rhode Island in the 1820s. They worked in factories and helped build the state's railroads. During the 1860s, people from Canada as well as Germany, Sweden, Portugal, and the Cape Verde Islands off the west coast of Africa made their way to the state.

Many of the Portuguese immigrants were skilled sailors. When they arrived in Newport and Providence during the 1860s, they found work on Rhode Island's whaling ships. Descendants of these workers still live in areas such as Providence's Fox Point community.

In the 1890s and early 1900s, immigrants arrived from Italy, Greece, Russia, Poland, Syria, Lithuania, Armenia, Lebanon, and the Ukraine. In the 1970s,

A Rhode Island father and son repair their sailboat together, honoring their state's long maritime tradition.

THE FRENCH CANADIANS OF WOONSOCKET

A large number of French Canadians moved to the northern city of Woonsocket during the mid-1800s. They left Quebec in Canada to work in Woonsocket's mills and factories, producing rubber, cotton cloth, and machines. Many of their descendants are still in Woonsocket. They often speak to one another in French. French Canadians make up Woonsocket's largest ethnic group today. Woonsocket's Museum of Work and Culture tells the story of French Canadian immigrants who came to work in the city.

many Hispanics began settling in Rhode Island. They have come from Puerto Rico and from such Spanish-speaking countries as Colombia, Mexico, the Dominican Republic, and Guatemala. In addition, Asians have moved to the state from countries such as Vietnam, Cambodia, and China. No matter where they are from, Rhode Islanders bring their cultures, religions, and traditions to enrich the state.

Rhode Island's Population Today

According to the 2010 U.S. Census, Rhode Island had 1,052,567 residents as of April 1 of that year. Among the states, Rhode Island ranks forty-third in population. Rhode Island is the second most crowded, or densely populated, state

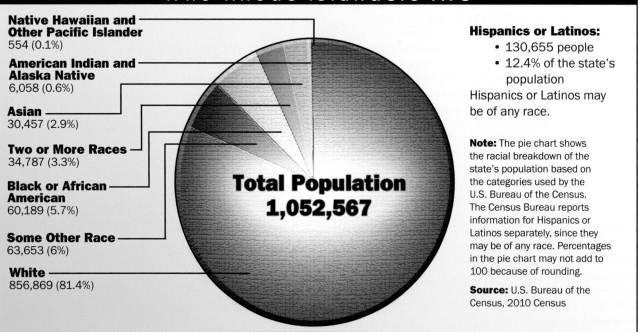

Who Rhode Islanders Are

Native Hawaiian and Other Pacific Islander
554 (0.1%)

American Indian and Alaska Native
6,058 (0.6%)

Asian
30,457 (2.9%)

Two or More Races
34,787 (3.3%)

Black or African American
60,189 (5.7%)

Some Other Race
63,653 (6%)

White
856,869 (81.4%)

**Total Population
1,052,567**

Hispanics or Latinos:
- 130,655 people
- 12.4% of the state's population

Hispanics or Latinos may be of any race.

Note: The pie chart shows the racial breakdown of the state's population based on the categories used by the U.S. Bureau of the Census. The Census Bureau reports information for Hispanics or Latinos separately, since they may be of any race. Percentages in the pie chart may not add to 100 because of rounding.

Source: U.S. Bureau of the Census, 2010 Census

Rhode Island is densely populated. In fact, the only state with more people per square mile is New Jersey.

in the country, however. An average of 1,018 people live in each square mile of land (393 people per sq km).

A lack of job opportunities has affected Rhode Island's population. In fact, Rhode Island is one of the slowest-growing states. Its population in 2010 had inched up by just 4,248 residents—a 0.4 percent increase—since 2000. The only state that grew slower than Rhode Island from 2000 to 2010 was Michigan.

Most people in Rhode Island reside in urban areas. Rhode Island's five most populous cities are Providence, Warwick, Cranston, Pawtucket, and East Providence. These cities are located in the eastern section of the state. The rest of Rhode Islanders are spread out among the small, outlying rural communities.

Becoming More Diverse

Most Rhode Islanders trace their ancestry to Europe. Over the years, however, people with other backgrounds have settled in the state.

Hispanic Americans make up the state's largest and fastest-growing cultural group. In 2000, there were 90,820 Hispanic Rhode Islanders. They made up 8.7 percent of the state's population. That number increased to 130,655 in 2010, when Hispanics made up 12.4 percent of the population. That is an increase of more than 40 percent. Many of Rhode Island's Hispanic residents live in communities in Providence, the state's capital and largest city. Today, African Americans comprise almost 6 percent of the state's population. The state's Asian population is nearly 3 percent.

Famous Rhode Islanders

Gilbert Stuart: Portrait Artist

Born in Saunderstown in 1755, Gilbert Stuart is considered the Father of American Portraiture. He is known for his portraits of U.S. presidents, including that of George Washington, which is featured on the U.S. one-dollar bill. Stuart painted more than a thousand portraits until his death in 1828. People can visit the Gilbert Stuart Birthplace and Museum in Saunderstown.

Kady Brownell: Civil War Soldier

Kady Brownell, born in South Africa in 1842, was living in Rhode Island when the Civil War began in 1861. When her husband joined a military unit called the Rhode Island Infantry, she signed up as well. She traveled with her husband's unit, became a fine sharpshooter, and learned to use a soldier's sword. As the troops marched into battle, Brownell carried the flag. She also helped injured soldiers and was often referred to as a Daughter of the Regiment. Brownell died in 1915.

Ida Lewis: Lighthouse Keeper

Ida Lewis was born in 1842 in Newport. Her father was a lighthouse keeper, but when he became ill in the 1850s, she took over the responsibilities of maintaining Lime Rock Light Station in Newport Harbor. She became known as the Bravest Woman in America for saving at least seventeen lives. Lewis finally became the official lighthouse keeper in 1879, and she served until her death in 1911. Lime Rock was eventually renamed the Ida Lewis Lighthouse.

Napoleon Lajoie: Baseball Player

Hall of Fame baseball player Napoleon "Nap" Lajoie was born in Woonsocket in 1874. He played for the Philadelphia Phillies, the Philadelphia Athletics, and the Cleveland Indians. Second baseman Lajoie is considered one of the greatest players of the American League in the early twentieth century. In 1901, he had the highest season batting average in American League history, an astounding .422. He was elected to the Baseball Hall of Fame in 1937. Lajoie died in 1959.

George M. Cohan: Composer, Actor, and Playwright

Thanks to George M. Cohan, musical comedy became a popular form of entertainment in America during the 1920s and 1930s. Born in Providence in 1878, Cohan was the first songwriter to be awarded the Congressional Medal of Honor, for composing the popular, troop-rallying World War I song "Over There." Other well-known Cohan-penned classics include "Yankee Doodle Dandy," "You're a Grand Old Flag," and "Give My Regards to Broadway." The talented entertainer died at his home in New York City in 1942.

Viola Davis: Actress

Award-winning actress Viola Davis was born in South Carolina in 1965. When she was an infant, her family moved to Central Falls, Rhode Island. She grew up in poverty there, but found her passion for acting in high school. Davis graduated from Rhode Island College with a major in theater and later attended the Juilliard School in New York City. She has won two Tony Awards for her theater work. Davis has starred in several films and was nominated for Academy Awards for her roles in *Doubt* and *The Help*.

American Indians

Before European settlement, the region's population was mostly American Indian. Today, however, American Indians number only about 6,000. About 2,400 belong to the Narragansett group. The tribe's headquarters are located on a reservation in Charlestown in southern Rhode Island.

The Narragansett Indians sued the state in the 1970s to regain their lands. They were awarded about 1,800 acres (700 hectares) near Charlestown. In 1983, they gained federal recognition as the Narragansett Indian Tribe of Rhode Island.

On the reservation, the tribe keeps its heritage alive through traditional crafts, songs, storytelling, an annual powwow, and other celebrations. People can also visit the Royal Indian Burial Ground in Charlestown. It is the resting place of many Narragansett sachems (chiefs) and their families.

Education

Education is important to Rhode Islanders. The state's public education system began in the 1820s. Today, many people work for the state's school system.

Some of Rhode Island's universities are also among the state's largest employers. The main campus of the state's public university—the University of Rhode Island (URI)—is located in Kingston. URI began as an agricultural school in 1888. Today, more than 19,000 students are enrolled there. The school has one of the nation's leading centers for ocean research and exploration.

This innovative public school in Pawtucket offers bilingual education in Spanish or Portuguese and English.

Providence is home to several colleges and universities, including the prestigious Brown University. Graduates include Horace Mann from the class of 1819, considered the father of American public education, and Charles Evans Hughes, who served as U.S. Supreme Court chief justice from 1930 to 1941. Other schools in Providence include Providence College, Johnson and Wales University (known for its culinary arts program), and the Rhode Island School of Design (RISD). RISD's Museum of Art contains an impressive collection of pieces from around the world as well as the work of African-American landscape artist Edward Mitchell Bannister, who painted in Rhode Island during the 1800s.

Located in Bristol is Roger Williams University. The school was named after Rhode Island's founder. Newport is home to Salve Regina University and the U.S. Naval War College, which trains naval officers.

Quick Facts

BROWN UNIVERSITY

Founded in 1764, Brown is the third-oldest college in New England and the seventh-oldest college in the United States. The institution, originally located in Warren and called the College of Rhode Island, moved to Providence in 1770. It was renamed Brown University in 1804 after businessman and 1786 graduate Nicholas Brown gave a gift totaling $5,000. Brown University began admitting women in 1891. More recently, Emma Watson, who rose to fame as Hermione in the *Harry Potter* films, has also attended Brown.

★ **Gaspee Days Colonial Encampment**

Each June, the city of Warwick commemorates the burning of the British customs ship *Gaspee* by Rhode Island colonists in 1772 with several events. At the encampment, visitors reenact military life during Rhode Island's colonial period. Dozens of people, dressed as soldiers in the American Revolution, camp out for the weekend. The festivities culminate with a symbolic burning of the *Gaspee*.

★ **Bristol Fourth of July Celebration**

Since 1785, Bristol has held the oldest continuous Fourth of July celebration in the United States. The popular event includes a parade, pageants, food, music, dancing, games, displays, and fireworks.

★ **Ancient and Horribles Parade**

Forget your typical Fourth of July parade. Since 1927, the Ancient and Horribles Parade has taken place each Independence Day in the town of Glocester. People wear wild and wacky outfits. They also decorate their cars and other vehicles in unusual ways. These types of parades date back to the 1870s or earlier in small New England towns.

★ **Black Ships Festival**

In 1854, Rhode Island's Commodore Matthew C. Perry negotiated a treaty with Japan opening up trade with the United States. Previously, foreign ships not permitted to enter the country were called Black Ships—or *kurofune* in Japanese. The Black Ships Festival, which takes place in Newport in July, honors the relations that Perry established with Japan. Among the many activities are a samurai sword exhibit, Japanese art displays, Japanese food, and martial arts demonstrations.

Newport Jazz Festival

The country's first jazz festival took place in Newport in 1954. The summer event attracts people from all over the world. Past performers have included jazz greats such as Louis Armstrong, Ella Fitzgerald, Duke Ellington, and Miles Davis.

Washington County Fair

Held in rural Richmond, this mid-August event is Rhode Island's largest agricultural fair. Among the many attractions are the farm museum, tractor pulls, crafts, New England food, and performances by country music artists.

International Quahog Festival

Clam lovers flock to this August festival, which pays tribute to the quahog clam. In addition to quahog chowder, visitors can try clam cakes, a stuffed, baked clam called a "stuffy," quahog chili, fried quahogs, and quahogs on the half shell.

Scituate Art Festival

This Columbus Day–weekend event takes place in the picturesque town of Scituate surrounded by beautiful fall foliage. It draws close to three hundred exhibitors specializing in painting, sculpture, antiques, and crafts.

Autumnfest

Since 1977, the northern city of Woonsocket has hosted this huge October event. The celebration includes amusement park rides and games, arts and crafts displays, spectacular fireworks, musical entertainment, and a parade.

Heritage Day Powwow

Held in Warwick, this November powwow displays Rhode Island's rich American Indian heritage. In addition to drumming, singing, and intertribal dances, there are arts, crafts, and storytelling.

How the Government Works

Rhode Island's current state constitution was adopted in 1843. Since then, it has been changed, or amended, more than forty times. Amendments to the constitution must be approved first by a majority vote in both houses of the state legislature, followed by a majority vote of the people in an election.

A state constitution describes how a state's government is organized and what powers the government has. A state constitution also limits the powers of government in order to protect the rights of individuals. Like the U.S. Constitution, the Rhode Island constitution divides its government into three separate branches to balance the power of each branch. The executive branch carries out state laws, the legislative branch makes new laws or changes existing ones, and the judicial branch interprets laws.

Quick Facts

RHODE ISLAND'S OFFICIAL NAME

Rhode Island may be the smallest state, but its official name is certainly the longest: the State of Rhode Island and Providence Plantations. Originally, only Aquidneck Island was called Rhode Island. Providence Plantations was the name used in the early 1600s for Providence and other towns in the present-day state. The 1663 charter from the king of England gave the area its lengthier name.

On the floor of the Rhode Island State House is the state seal with the state motto: *Hope.*

Like the U.S. Capitol in Washington, D.C., the Rhode Island State House has a large central dome and two wings. Each chamber of the legislature meets in its own wing.

State Government

A governor, elected to a four-year term, heads the state. Rhode Island is one of the few states that does not have an official governor's residence. Rhode Island's legislature is called the general assembly. It is made up of two houses, or chambers, a senate and a house of representatives. Senators and representatives represent specific regions of the state.

The state government is responsible for issues that affect the state. The job of state officials includes drafting, approving, and enforcing laws, as well as managing state budgets. The state government also handles issues with other states, as well as with the federal government in Washington, D.C.

Rhode Island's state government is centered in its capital, Providence. State lawmakers meet inside the capitol, called the Rhode Island State House. The governor, lieutenant governor, secretary of state, general treasurer, and other officials work here as well.

RHODE ISLAND STATE HOUSE DOME
The Rhode Island State House has the fourth-largest unsupported marble dome in the world. On top of the massive dome stands Independent Man. Measuring 11 feet (3 m) tall, the gold-covered bronze statue weighs 500 pounds (230 kg). The statue represents the independent spirit that led Roger Williams to settle Rhode Island.

Building began on the Rhode Island State House in 1895. Inside the building is a vault that contains the Royal Charter of 1663 from King Charles II of England. The charter guaranteed Rhode Island's settlers freedom of religion and freedom to govern their own colony. Hanging in the Rhode Island State House is the famous painting of George Washington by Rhode Island's Gilbert Stuart.

Representation in Washington, D.C.

At the national level, Rhode Island has representatives in both houses of the U.S. Congress. Each state elects two U.S. senators, who serve six-year terms. There is no limit on the number of terms a U.S. senator can serve. A state's population determines the number of people that it sends to the U.S. House

CLAIBORNE PELL

Claiborne Pell (1918–2009) was a U.S. senator from Rhode Island for more than three decades. He served six terms, from 1961 to 1997. The senator is best known for creating the Pell Grant, which provides financial aid to college students in need.

of Representatives. Rhode Islanders elect two representatives to the House. They serve two-year terms and can be reelected an unlimited number of times.

Local Government

Rhode Island is divided into five counties—Providence, Kent, Washington, Bristol, and Newport. There is, however, no county government. The main units of local government within the state are its thirty-nine municipalities. They are made up of eight cities and thirty-one towns. The majority of these municipalities are presided over by a mayor and a city or town council.

As in other states, many towns in Rhode Island hold annual town meetings. These meetings originated during the colonial era, and all eligible voters can attend. At these sessions, voters can approve local spending, pass laws, and even elect local officials.

How a Bill Becomes a Law

State laws often start out as the ideas of concerned residents. Any Rhode Islander can talk to his or her state

COUNTY CAPITALS

Rhode Island once had five state capitals—one for each county. In 1854, the number was reduced to two—Providence and Newport. In 1900, Providence became the sole capital.

Branches of Government

EXECUTIVE ★ ★ ★ ★ ★ ★ ★ ★

The governor heads the executive branch. The governor carries out the laws that the legislative branch passes. Rhode Island's voters elect a governor every four years. The governor may serve only two terms in a row. Other executive branch officials include the lieutenant governor (who takes over if the governor can no longer serve), attorney general, secretary of state, and general treasurer. Each of these officials is voted into office to serve a four-year term. Like the governor, these elected officials cannot serve more than two terms in a row.

LEGISLATIVE ★ ★ ★ ★ ★ ★ ★ ★

Rhode Island's legislative branch is called the general assembly. It is made up of a senate with thirty-eight members and a house of representatives with seventy-five members. Members of both houses earn their jobs through popular elections, and each serves a two-year term. Rhode Island's general assembly is responsible for making the state's laws and approving people nominated by the governor to be justices of the state's supreme court.

JUDICIAL ★ ★ ★ ★ ★ ★ ★ ★

Rhode Island's judicial branch interprets and applies the state's laws. The state's highest court is the supreme court. It is made up of a chief justice and four associate justices. The governor nominates justices from a list submitted by a judicial nominating committee. The nominee then must be approved by the general assembly. If approved, the justices are appointed to life terms. The state's main trial court is the superior court. It consists of twenty-two judges whom the governor chooses with the senate's approval. In addition, Rhode Island has family, district, municipal, and probate courts. The governor, with the consent of the senate, appoints these judges. More serious criminal and civil cases are sent to the superior court, which also hears appeals of district court decisions.

legislators about issues that affect the state and its residents. If a resident—or a group of residents—has a suggestion for a new law, it can be presented to a state legislator. Often, the legislator will develop the idea into a bill (a proposed law). The bill is then presented to the legislator's chamber of the general assembly. If the legislator is a senator, the bill is brought first to the

Visitors to the Rhode Island State House watch the opening of the 2012 legislative session from the house gallery.

senate. If the legislator is a state representative, the bill is brought to the house of representatives.

The bill gets a specific number to identify it. The numbered bill then goes to a committee of legislators for review. The committee members read and discuss the bill. If they agree with it, they can recommend that the bill is passed as it is. If the bill is not recommended, it does not move forward. The committee can also make changes, refer the bill to another committee, or recommend that the discussion of the bill should be postponed. The committee may also present the bill to fellow legislators without comment.

If the bill is recommended for passage, it is discussed by the full senate or full house. Changes may be made or the bill might remain the same. If the legislators of one house approve the bill, it goes to the other chamber for approval. Once there, the bill follows the same process until it is approved. If the senate and the house approve two different versions of the same bill, a conference committee that includes members of both houses meets to resolve the differences. The committee ultimately creates a final version of the bill for approval by both chambers of the general assembly.

A bill that has been approved by both houses in exactly the same form is then sent to the governor. The governor can approve the bill by signing it, and the bill becomes a law. He or she can also allow the bill to become law without signing it. If the governor disagrees with the bill, he or she can veto (reject) it. Even if a bill is vetoed, it still has a chance to become law if three-fifths of the members of both houses of the legislature vote again to approve it. This is called overriding the governor's veto.

Contacting Lawmakers

★ ★ ★ ★ ★ ★ ★ ★ ★ ★ ★ ★

Rhode Islanders can take an active role in government and contact their representative and senator about issues of concern. To find contact information for Rhode Island's state legislators, go to

https://sos.ri.gov/vic

Enter your street and zip code or city or town to find your senator and representative.

Making a Living

Throughout Rhode Island's history, its people have found ways to survive on the land. For many years, farming, raising livestock, and fishing in the rivers, bays, and ocean were major ways that residents made a living. Over time, however, manufacturing and service industries grew in importance. Service industries are those in which workers provide a service to others rather than produce goods. An important service industry in Rhode Island today involves meeting the needs of the many tourists who visit the state each year. In the twenty-first century, Rhode Islanders are also focused on bringing emerging jobs in biotechnology and other high-tech fields to the state to bolster its economy.

Manufacturing

After Samuel Slater built his water-powered cotton mill in Pawtucket, Rhode Island quickly became a manufacturing giant. Textile mills were soon lining the state's rivers. During the entire nineteenth and early twentieth centuries, manufacturing was the most profitable industry in Rhode Island. More than half the state's workforce was employed in factories and mills. Today, however, there are fewer manufacturing jobs in the state. Although many factories have closed or relocated, the manufacturing industry still employs about 57,000 people. Those workers make up nearly 12 percent of the state's labor force.

Fresh produce and other foods from local farms are for sale at the Hope Street Farmers Market in Providence.

Workers & Industries

Industry	Number of People Working in That Industry	Percentage of All Workers Who Are Working in That Industry
Education and health care	127,846	26%
Wholesale and retail businesses	75,987	15.5%
Publishing, media, entertainment, hotels, and restaurants	62,378	12.8%
Manufacturing	56,778	11.6%
Professionals, scientists, and managers	46,298	9.4%
Banking and finance, insurance, and real estate	34,819	7.1%
Construction	24,242	4.9%
Government	24,015	4.9%
Other services	20,103	4.1%
Transportation and public utilities	17,232	3.5%
Farming, fishing, forestry, and mining	1,266	0.3%
Totals	**490,964**	**100%**

Notes: Figures above do not include people in the armed forces.
"Professionals" includes people such as doctors and lawyers.
Percentages may not add to 100 because of rounding.

Source: U.S. Bureau of the Census, 2010 estimates

An assembly-line worker coils copper tubing at a Rhode Island plant.

Rhode Island manufactures metal products such as nuts, bolts, wires, tools, and machine parts. Other leading manufactured products include chemicals, plastics, textiles, transportation equipment, electronic equipment, and scientific equipment—particularly medical and surgical products. Yachts, boats, and some submarine parts are also made in Rhode Island. In addition, Rhode Island is known for producing jewelry and silverware. Providence is home to many jewelry manufacturing companies.

Agriculture, Livestock, and Fishing

Farming, raising livestock, and fishing make up a very small part of Rhode Island's economy today. Less than one percent of Rhode Island's labor force works in these areas. The state has about 1,200 farms.

Rhode Island's top farm products are nursery and greenhouse plants. These include flowering plants, Christmas trees, grass sod, and decorative trees and shrubs. Milk and other dairy products are other main agricultural commodities. Rhode Island farm crops include potatoes, sweet corn, tomatoes, and squash. Rhode Island's orchards grow fruits such as apples, peaches, pears, and berries.

Farmers raise different types of livestock, including dairy cows, hogs, and hens. The products that come from the livestock are often processed or prepared in the state. The Rhode Island red (the state bird) is a special breed of chicken raised in Little Compton.

Fishing is not as large an industry as it once was. But fishing boats in towns and villages such as Galilee along the Narragansett Bay bring in flounder, cod, tuna, squid, scallops, and whiting. Rhode Island fishers also harvest clams and lobsters.

Rhode Island's seafood industry is threatened by pollution in Narragansett Bay, where most of the state's fishing takes place. State sewage treatment plants that were built in the 1800s are no longer effective. After a heavy rainfall, water tends to fill up the treatment plants, causing an overflow of sewage into the bay. This sewage is harming the fish and other sea creatures, affecting the state's fishing industry. From finding ways to fix the treatment plants to establishing new rules about the amount of sewage that can be processed or stored, environmental groups and concerned citizens are working to reduce pollution in the bay.

Fishing boats in Rhode Island bring in a variety of fish and shellfish.

RECIPE FOR JOHNNYCAKES

Rhode Island is famous for its johnnycakes. These traditional Rhode Island pancakes are made from cornmeal instead of flour. Rhode Island's early settlers learned to make them from the area's American Indians. Since johnnycakes could be eaten hot or cold on long trips, they were likely originally called "journey cakes."

WHAT YOU NEED

1 cup (160 g) cornmeal

1 teaspoon (4 g) sugar

$1/2$ teaspoon (3 g) salt

$1 \, 1/4$ cups (300 milliliters) boiling water

Shortening or butter

To make the pancake batter, first mix the cornmeal, sugar, and salt in a bowl. Next, boil the water. Have an adult help you with the stove. Let the water cool a bit and then pour it over the dry ingredients in the bowl. The mixture should be mushy but not watery.

Put a little shortening or butter on a pancake griddle or frying pan. Heat the pan until the butter or shortening is melted. Then drop a few spoonfuls of the batter onto the pan.

Fry the batter over medium heat for about 2 minutes before turning it over with a spatula. Cook the other side for about 2 minutes. The cakes should be a golden-brown color. Serve plain or topped with butter, honey, maple syrup, or powdered sugar.

Service Industries

To make up for the decline of manufacturing and to help improve Rhode Island's economy, state officials began, in the 1970s, to try to attract service industries to the region. Today, most of Rhode Island's economy is made up of service jobs, particularly in health care and education. About 26 percent of the state's workforce is employed in health care or education. The state hopes to make itself a center of these growing fields, which it has dubbed "meds and eds."

Health services, the state's largest industry, include doctors' offices, hospitals, and walk-in clinics. In 2011, Brown University opened a new medical school (the only one in the state) about 1 mile (1.6 km) from its main campus in Providence.

Those who perform educational services, such as teachers and school administrators, also make up a sizable portion of the service industry. So do people who work in finance, insurance, and real estate. Cities such as Providence and Warwick host the headquarters for a number of large banks and other financial institutions.

Quick Facts

NARRAGANSETT PACER

The Rhode Island red chicken is not the only animal created by state breeders. In the late 1600s, the Narragansett pacer—the first North American horse breed—was developed in Rhode Island. Used for racing and riding, the horse is extinct today. George Washington owned a Narragansett pacer. It is also believed to be the horse that Paul Revere rode on his famous midnight ride in 1775 to warn American colonists that the British were coming.

Quick Facts

NEWPORT FIRSTS

Many leisure and entertainment-related activities trace their origins to historic Newport. In 1774, the city hosted the first circus to perform in what is now the United States. The first polo match played in the United States took place in Newport in 1876. Five years later, Newport was the site of the first U.S. National Lawn Tennis Championship (the tournament that is now the U.S. Open). In 1895, the United States Golf Association held the first U.S. Open Championship in Newport.

Shoppers walk in the Arcade in Providence. Originally built in 1828, the Arcade is the oldest indoor shopping mall in the United States.

Products & Resources

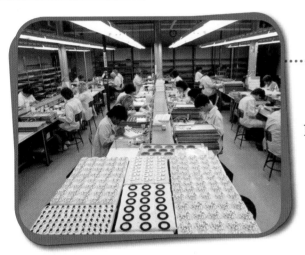

Metal Products

Rhode Island is known for jewelry, silverware, and other goods made out of precious metals such as silver. Some factories in the state still create these products. Factories and plants also manufacture tools and metal products for construction, electrical equipment, and computer parts.

Agricultural Products

Rhode Island farms yield a variety of agricultural products, ranging from flowering plants, decorative trees, and shrubs, to a variety of fruits and vegetables. Farms in Rhode Island also produce hay.

Toys

One of the world's largest toy makers, Hasbro, was founded in Rhode Island. Headquartered in Pawtucket, Hasbro today employs about six thousand people worldwide. In 1923, brothers Henry and Helal Hassenfeld first started the company in Providence, selling items such as textiles and school supplies. In the 1940s, the company's first toys were doctor and nurse kits. Its first hit toy, in the 1950s, was Mr. Potato Head. Today's popular Hasbro toys include Transformers robot toys and the Monopoly board game.

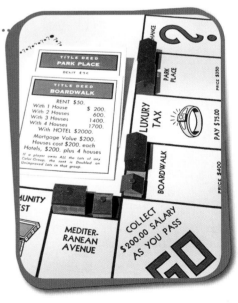

Seafood

Commercial fishing boats go into Rhode Island's coastal waters to catch a wide range of fish. They also harvest shellfish and other sea animals. Many Rhode Islanders work in the factories and plants that clean, process, and pack these seafood products. The products are often shipped out to markets around the country and throughout the world.

Tourism

For a small state, Rhode Island has many things that attract millions of tourists every year. For those who like summer activities such as swimming, boating, and fishing, the state's numerous sandy beaches and ocean-side resorts are especially attractive. Rhode Island's rich history, with historical sites and museums, also draws people to the state. Tourists spend about $5 billion each year in Rhode Island.

Scientific Instruments

Rhode Island manufacturers supply the health industry with many useful tools. Doctors and health care workers around the country use items manufactured in the state, such as syringes (needles used to draw blood) and devices that measure blood pressure.

Tourism

Tourism is a major contributor to the state's economy, supporting more than 70,000 jobs in Rhode Island. It is also the state's fastest-growing industry.

The coastal town of Newport draws people from around the world. Its grand mansions are among its most popular destinations. One mansion, Rosecliff, completed in 1902, was modeled after Versailles, the palace of kings in France. Newport's Cliff Walk offers stunning ocean views. In the heart of Newport is the Brick Market Place, filled with shops and restaurants. Nearby is St. Mary's, the oldest Roman Catholic parish in Rhode Island.

Newport also hosts world-famous sporting events. From 1930 to 1983, it was home to the America's Cup yacht races. Every two years in mid-June, the Newport Bermuda Yacht Race is held. Beginning in Newport, boaters race

The 3.5-mile (5.6-km) Cliff Walk borders the water on one side and, on the other, the grounds of many of Newport's stately mansions.

635 nautical miles (1,175 km) across the ocean to the island of Bermuda. For tennis lovers, the International Tennis Hall of Fame on Newport's historic Bellevue Avenue is open to the public.

During the summer, Newport's annual jazz, folk, and classical musical festivals attract large crowds and talented performers. The jazz and folk festivals take place at Fort Adams in Newport. Now a state park, Fort Adams was a military base until the 1950s. The classical musical festival is held in some of Newport's mansions.

Several nights a year Providence hosts WaterFire. About eighty sparkling bonfires are set ablaze in baskets along three rivers that pass through the middle of the capital city. History lovers are often found on Providence's Benefit Street. Visitors can tour the area nicknamed the Mile of History for its beautifully restored colonial homes, churches, and museums. Stephen Hopkins's home is located near Benefit Street. Hopkins signed the Declaration of Independence and was Rhode Island's colonial governor from 1755 to 1767.

South of Providence is Warwick—Rhode Island's second-largest city. Warwick is known as the retail capital of Rhode Island. Warwick is also home to Rhode Island's main airport, T.F. Green International Airport.

Visitors to Block Island can tour the Southeast Lighthouse.

Farther south, ferries transport people from the fishing village of Galilee to Block Island. The island's quaint inns and serene beaches are not the only draws. Each fall, bird-watchers come to see songbirds that stop on the island on their journey south.

Those wanting to "spin" around Rhode Island can check out the state's many merry-go-rounds. Built in 1876, the Flying Horse Carousel in Westerly may be the oldest in the country. The twenty hand-carved wooden horses are suspended from chains and swing, or "fly out," as the carousel turns.

From its carousels and colonial homes to its developing high-tech, health care, and research industries, Rhode Island has much to offer. The state may have a reputation for being small, but it is certainly big when it comes to possibilities for the future.

Quick Facts

GREEN ANIMALS

Where can you find shrubs shaped like giraffes, teddy bears, and elephants? Take a trip to the Green Animals Topiary Garden in Portsmouth. Topiaries are sculptured trees and bushes. Green Animals, one of the oldest gardens of its kind in the country, has more than eighty topiaries, dating from 1905, on display.

State Flag & Seal

Rhode Island's state flag features a golden anchor on a white background. Thirteen golden stars, encircling the anchor, represent the original thirteen colonies. Underneath the anchor is a blue ribbon with the word Hope in gold. This version of the flag was adopted in 1897.

The state seal depicts a golden anchor with the word Hope above it. Written along the circular border of the seal are the words Seal of the State of Rhode Island and Providence Plantations 1636. "1636" represents the year Roger Williams first established Rhode Island's first permanent European settlement. The seal was adopted in 1664.

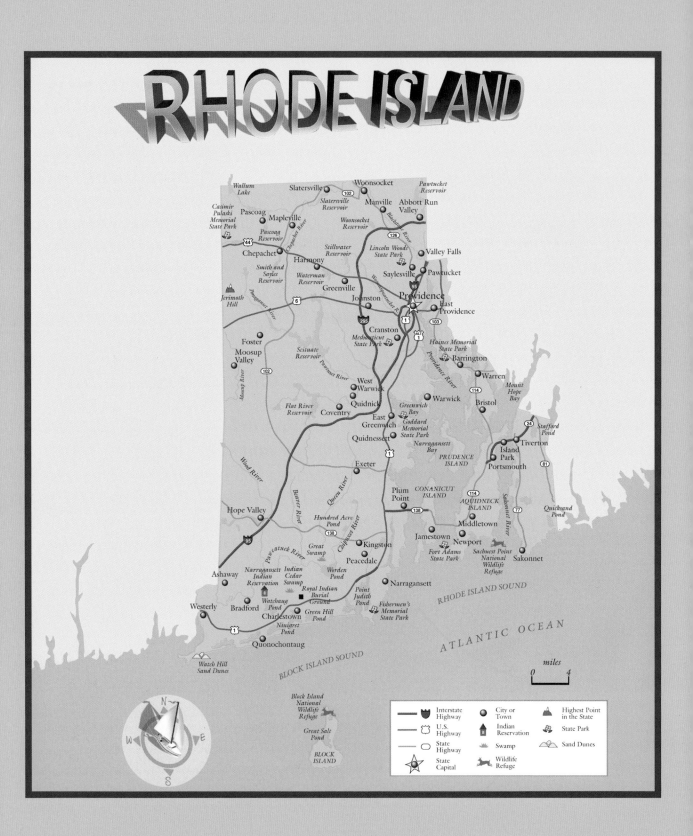

RHODE ISLAND

Wallum Lake
Slatersville
Woonsocket
Pawtucket Reservoir
Casimir Pulaski Memorial State Park
Pascoag
Mapleville
Slatersville Reservoir
Manville
Abbott Run Valley
Pascoag Reservoir
Woonsocket Reservoir
Chepachet
Harmony
Stillwater Reservoir
Lincoln Woods State Park
Valley Falls
Smith and Sayles Reservoir
Waterman Reservoir
Saylesville
Pawtucket
Greenville
Jerimoth Hill
Johnston
Providence
East Providence
Foster
Cranston
Meshanticut State Park
Haines Memorial State Park
Barrington
Moosup Valley
Scituate Reservoir
West Warwick
Warren
Mount Hope Bay
Quidnick
Warwick
Bristol
Flat River Reservoir
Coventry
East Greenwich
Greenwich Bay
Goddard Memorial State Park
Stafford Pond
Tiverton
Quidnessett
Narragansett Bay
Island Park
Portsmouth
Exeter
Plum Point
CONANICUT ISLAND
PRUDENCE ISLAND
AQUIDNECK ISLAND
Hope Valley
Hundred Acre Pond
Middletown
Quicksand Pond
Jamestown
Newport
Sakonnet
Great Swamp
Kingston
Fort Adams State Park
Sachuest Point National Wildlife Refuge
Ashaway
Narragansett Indian Reservation
Indian Cedar Swamp
Worden Pond
Peacedale
Royal Indian Burial Ground
Narragansett
Westerly
Bradford
Watchaug Pond
Green Hill Pond
Point Judith Pond
Fishermen's Memorial State Park
RHODE ISLAND SOUND
Charlestown
Ninigret Pond
Quonochontaug
ATLANTIC OCEAN
Watch Hill Sand Dunes
BLOCK ISLAND SOUND

miles
0   4

Block Island National Wildlife Refuge

Great Salt Pond

BLOCK ISLAND

Legend

Interstate Highway	City or Town	Highest Point in the State
U.S. Highway	Indian Reservation	State Park
State Highway	Swamp	Sand Dunes
State Capital	Wildlife Refuge	

State Song

Rhode Island

words and music by Thomas Clarke Brown

NOTE: "Rhode Island" is the state's official state march. It was adopted in 1996.

BOOKS

Burgan, Michael. *Roger Williams: Founder of Rhode Island.* Minneapolis: Compass Point, 2006.

Dell, Pamela. *The Wampanoag* (First Americans). Tarrytown, NY: Marshall Cavendish Benchmark, 2009.

McDermott, Jesse. *Voices from Colonial America: Rhode Island 1636–1776.* Washington, D.C.: National Geographic Children's Books, 2006.

Moss, Marissa. *The Bravest Woman in America.* New York: Random House, 2011.

Slavicek, Louise Chipley. *Anne Hutchinson* (Leaders of the Colonial Era). New York: Chelsea House, 2011.

WEBSITES

Narragansett Indian Tribe:
http://www.narragansett-tribe.org

Newport Mansions:
http://www.newportmansions.org

Official Site of the State of Rhode Island:
http://www.ri.gov

Visit Rhode Island:
http://www.visitrhodeisland.com

Rick Petreycik is a writer whose articles on history, music, film, and business have appeared in *American Legacy, Rolling Stone, Yankee, Disney Magazine,* and the *Hartford Courant,* among other publications. He lives in Connecticut with his wife, Pattilee, and daughter, Caitlin.

Lisa M. Herrington is a former executive managing editor at *Weekly Reader.* The Ocean State has a special place in her heart. Growing up, she spent many summer vacations with her family visiting Narragansett, Newport, Point Judith, and Block Island. Her favorite memories include touring the Breakers and Hammersmith Farm, eating Rhode Island clam cakes, and enjoying the spectacular ocean views along Newport's Cliff Walk. Herrington lives in neighboring Connecticut with her husband, Ryan, and daughter, Caroline.

★ INDEX ★

Page numbers in **boldface** are illustrations.